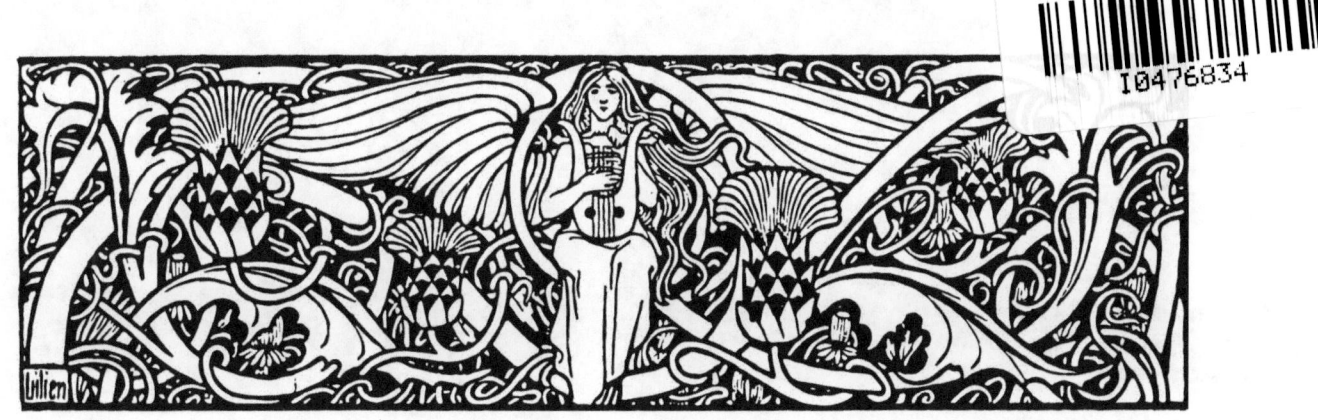

Masters of Illustration
Adult Coloring Book

Featuring the illustrations of
John Austen
Aubrey Beardsley
Ivan Bilibin
Harry Clarke
Henry Justice Ford
Joseph René Gockinga
William Heath Robinson
John Tenniel

Compiled and edited by
Elle Zissou

John Austen
English Illustrator
1886-1948

This illustration is from *Sheherezade.*

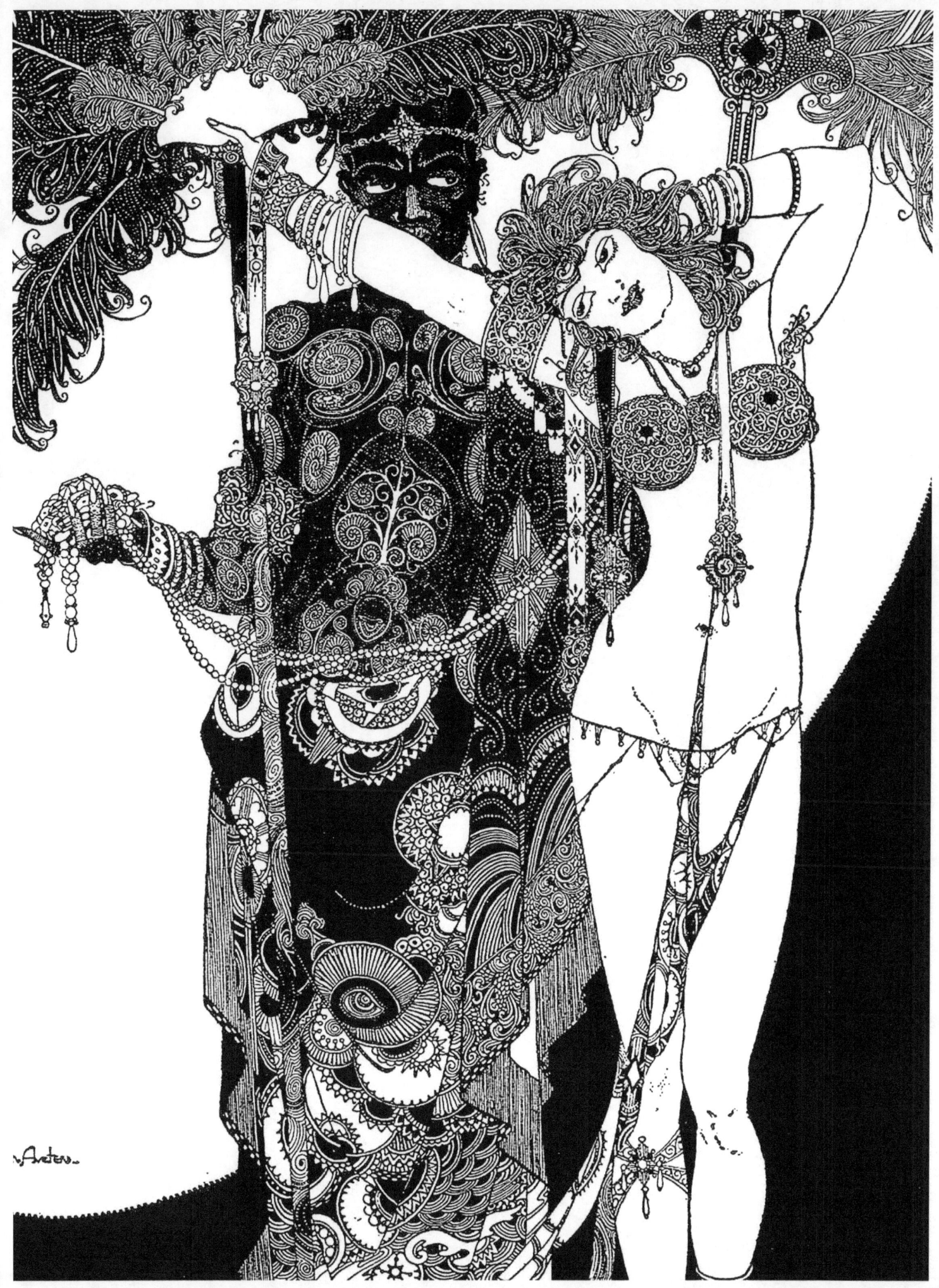

John Austen
English Illustrator
1886-1948

This illustration is from *Hamlet*.

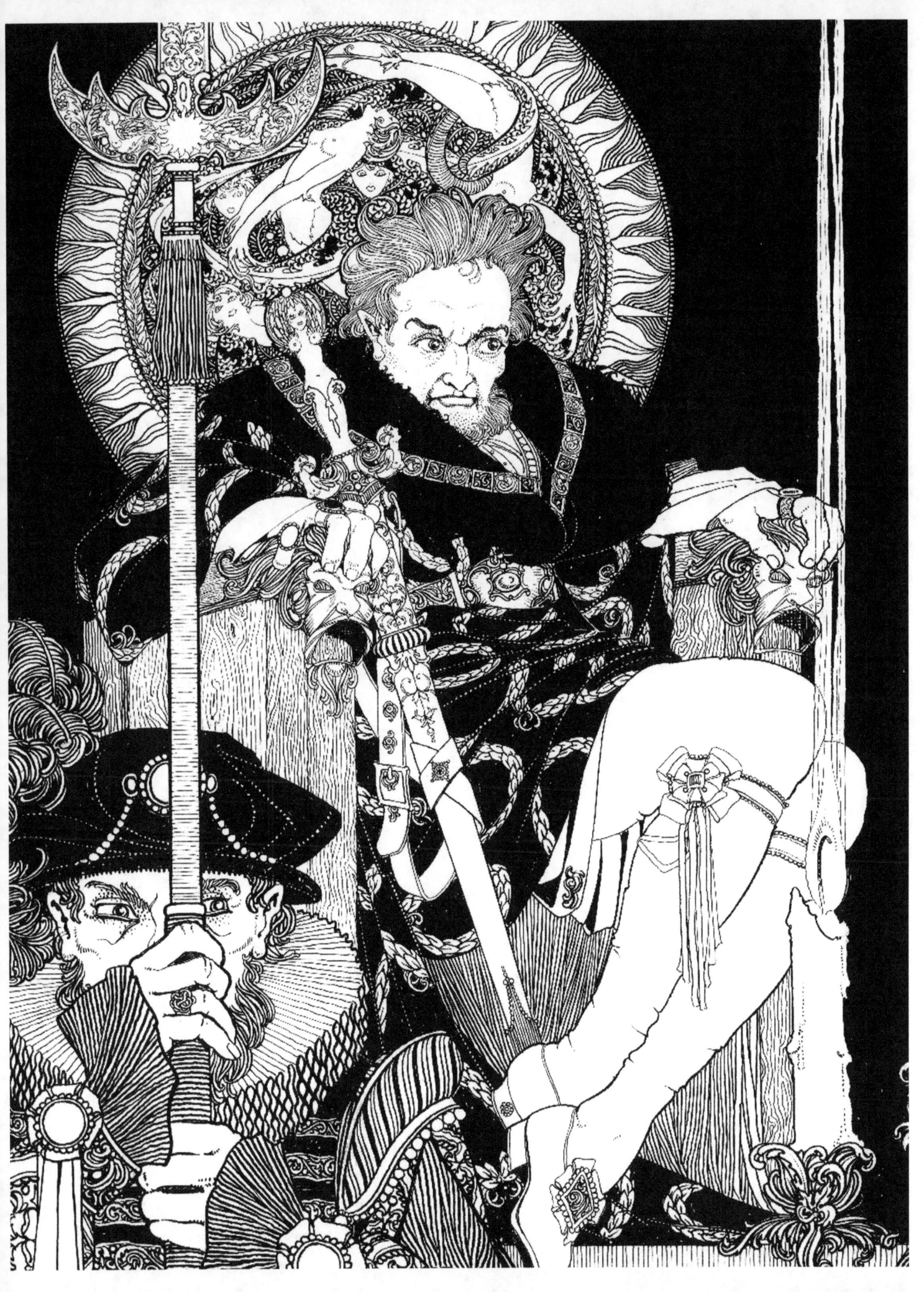

John Austen
English Illustrator
1886-1948

This illustration is from *Hamlet*.

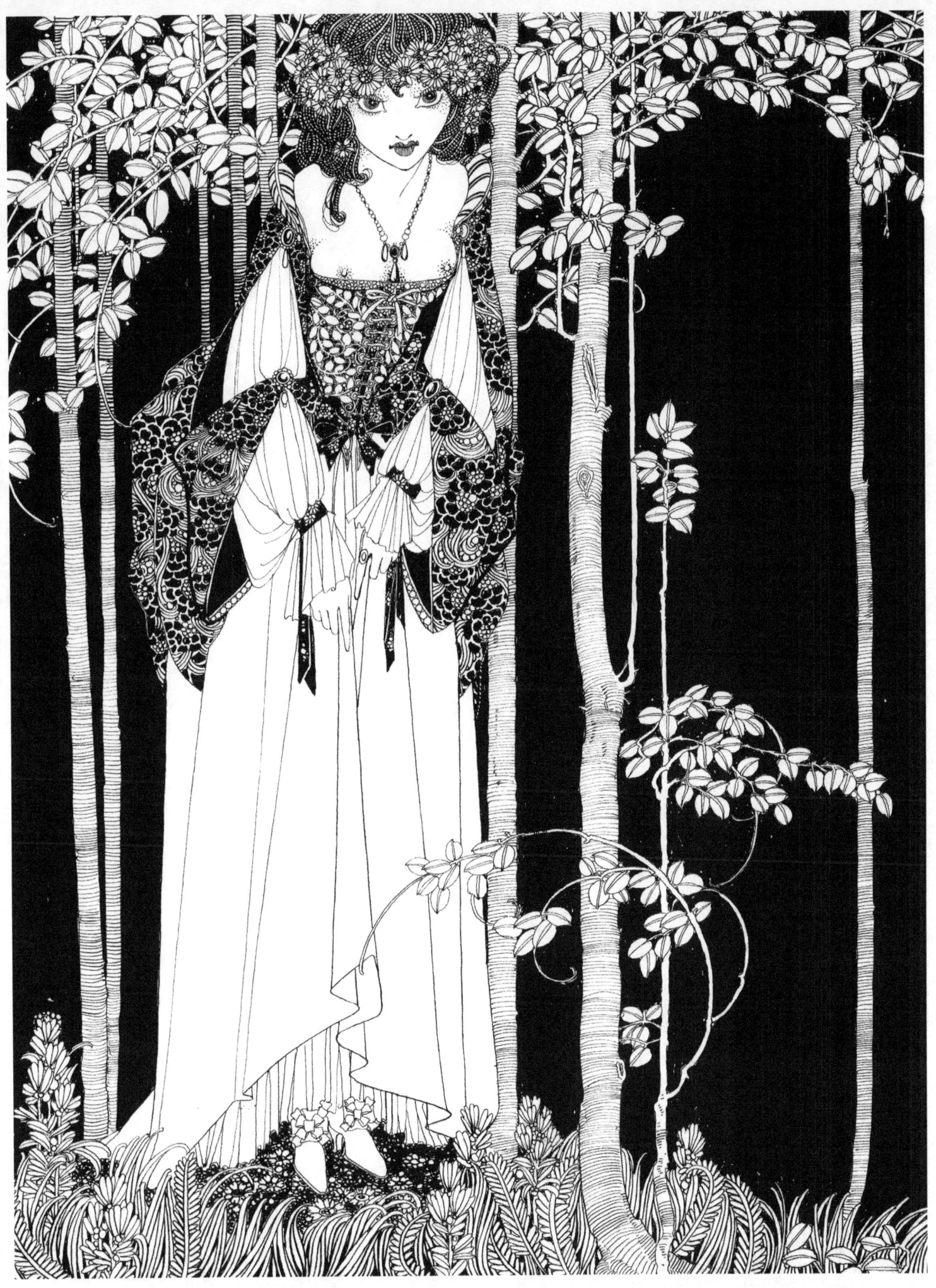

Aubrey Beardsley
English Illustrator and Author
1872-1898

Illustration for 'The Rape of the Lock'
by Alexander Pope

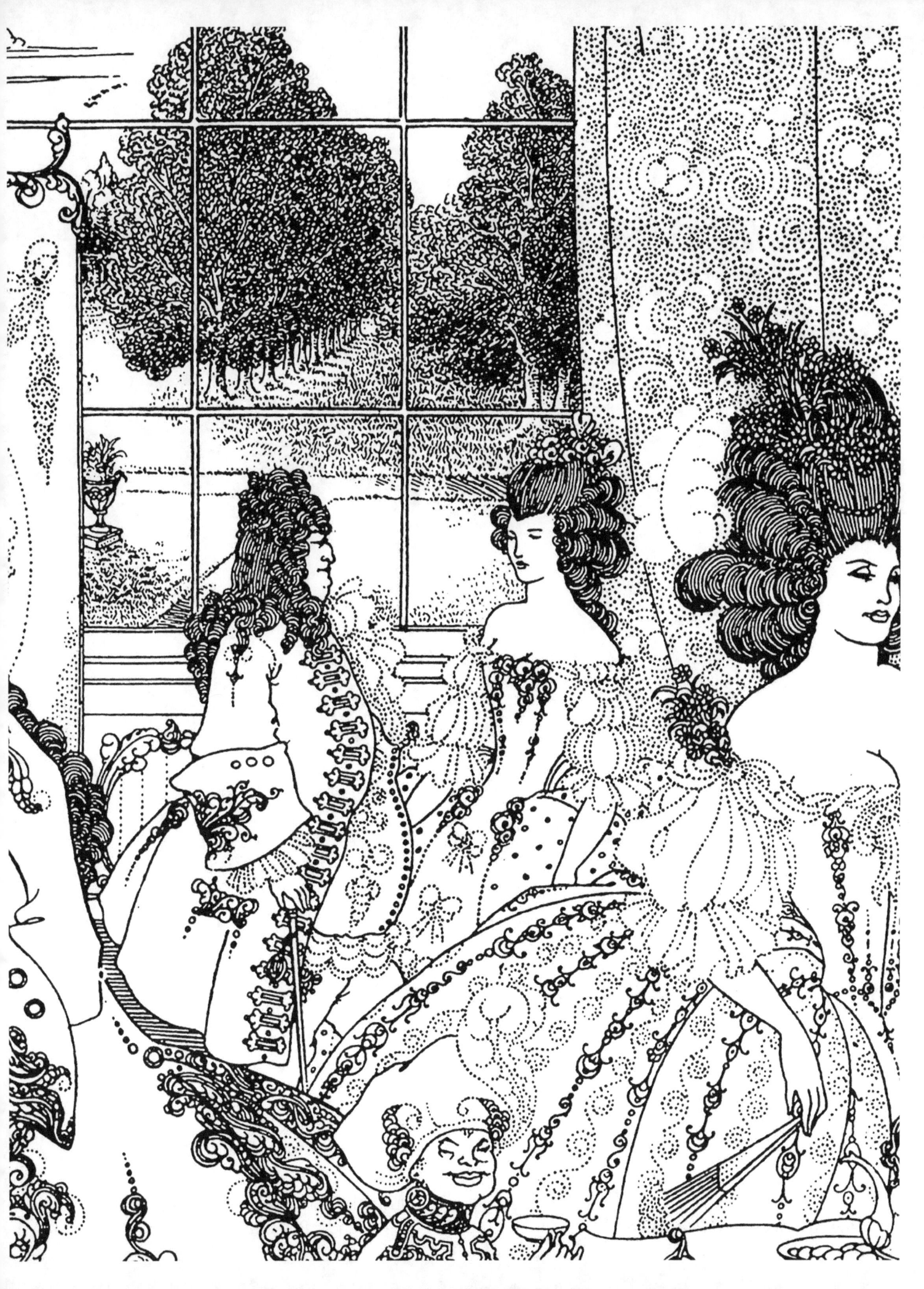

Aubrey Beardsley
English Illustrator and Author
1872-1898

Illustration for 'The Rape of the Lock'
by Alexander Pope

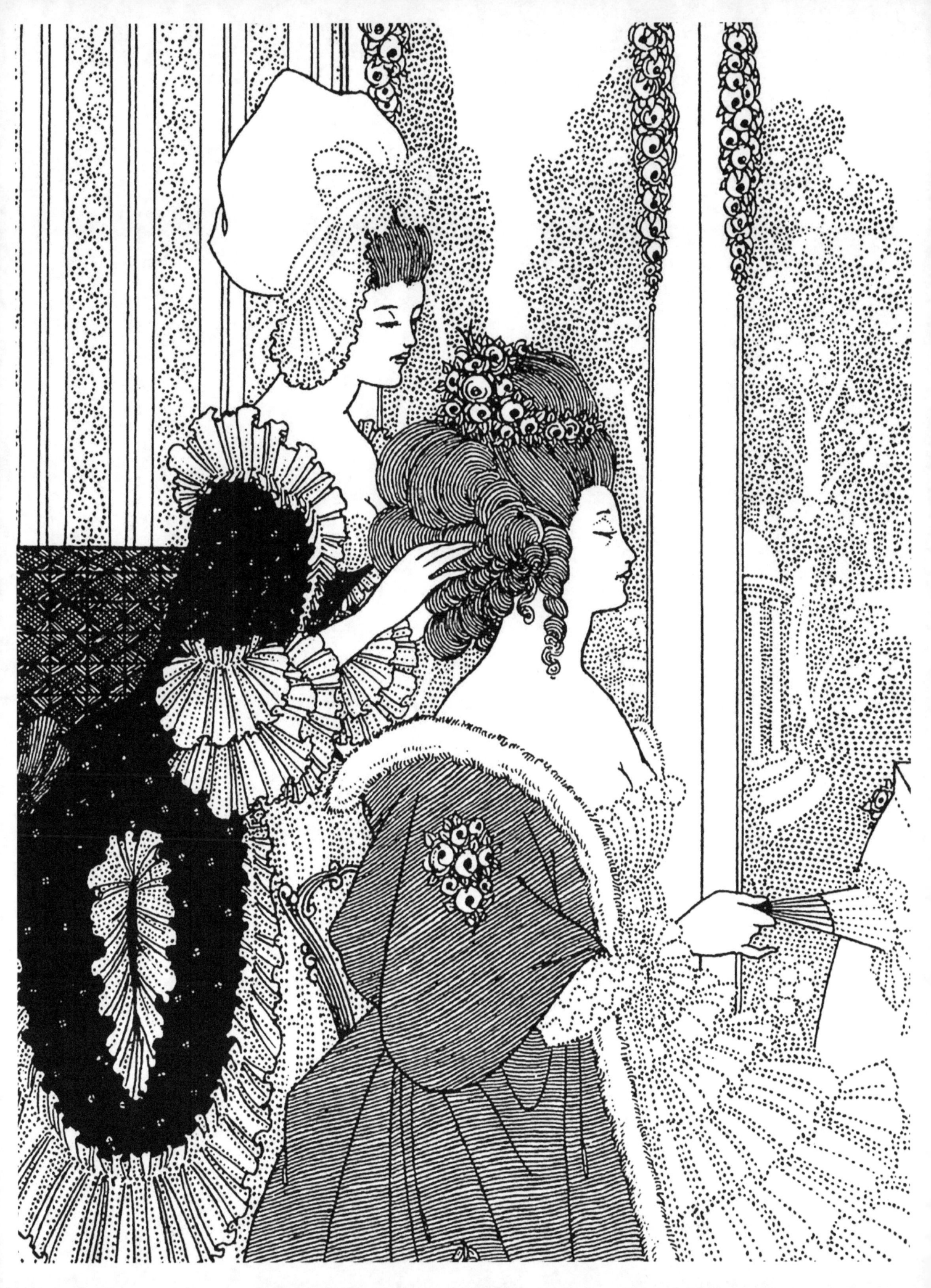

Aubrey Beardsley
English Illustrator and Author
1872-1898

Illustration for 'The Toilet of Salome"

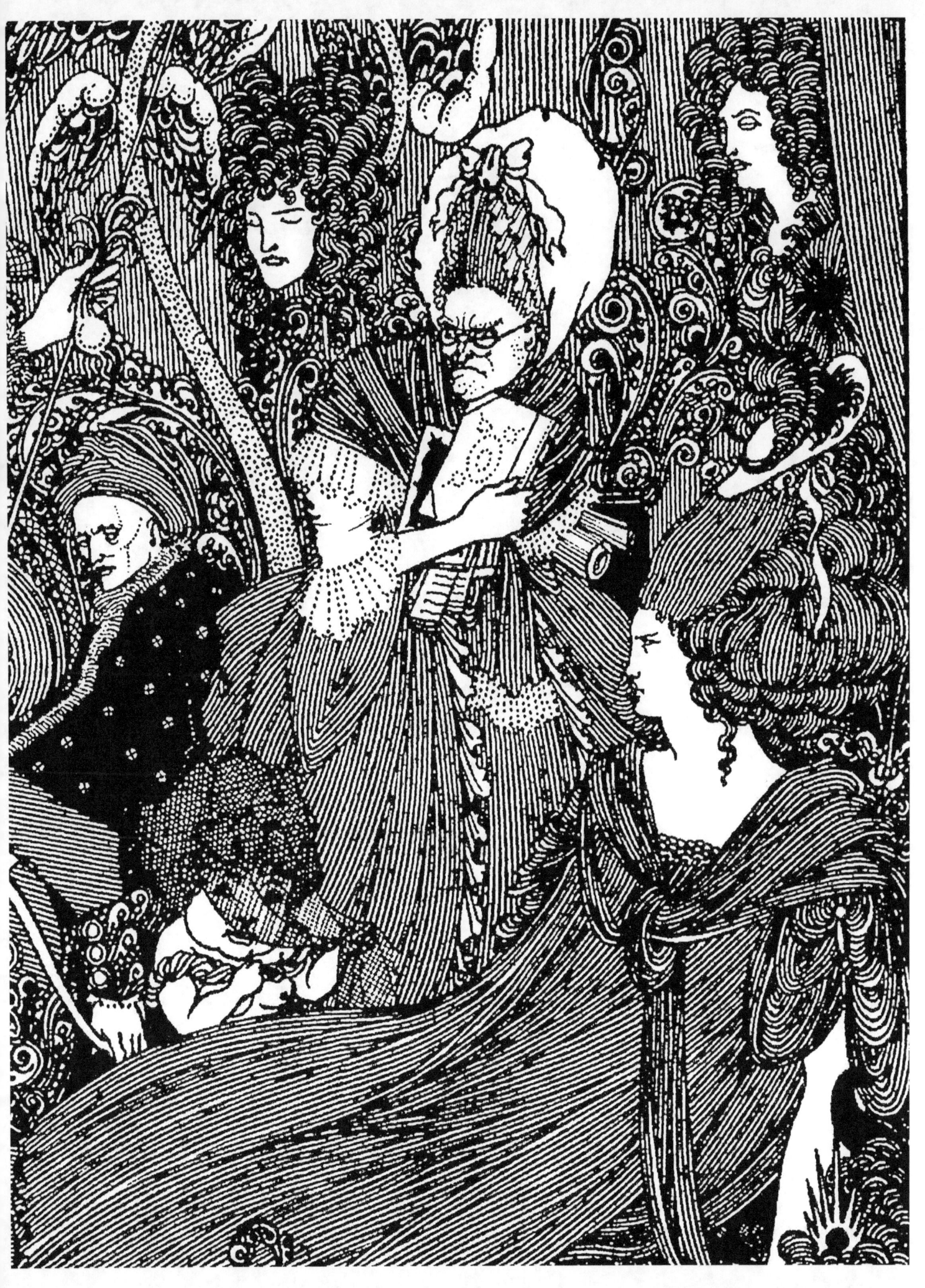

Ivan Bilibin
Russian Illustrator and Stage Director
1876-1942

Illustration for the epic "Ilya Muromets and
Svyatogor's wife".

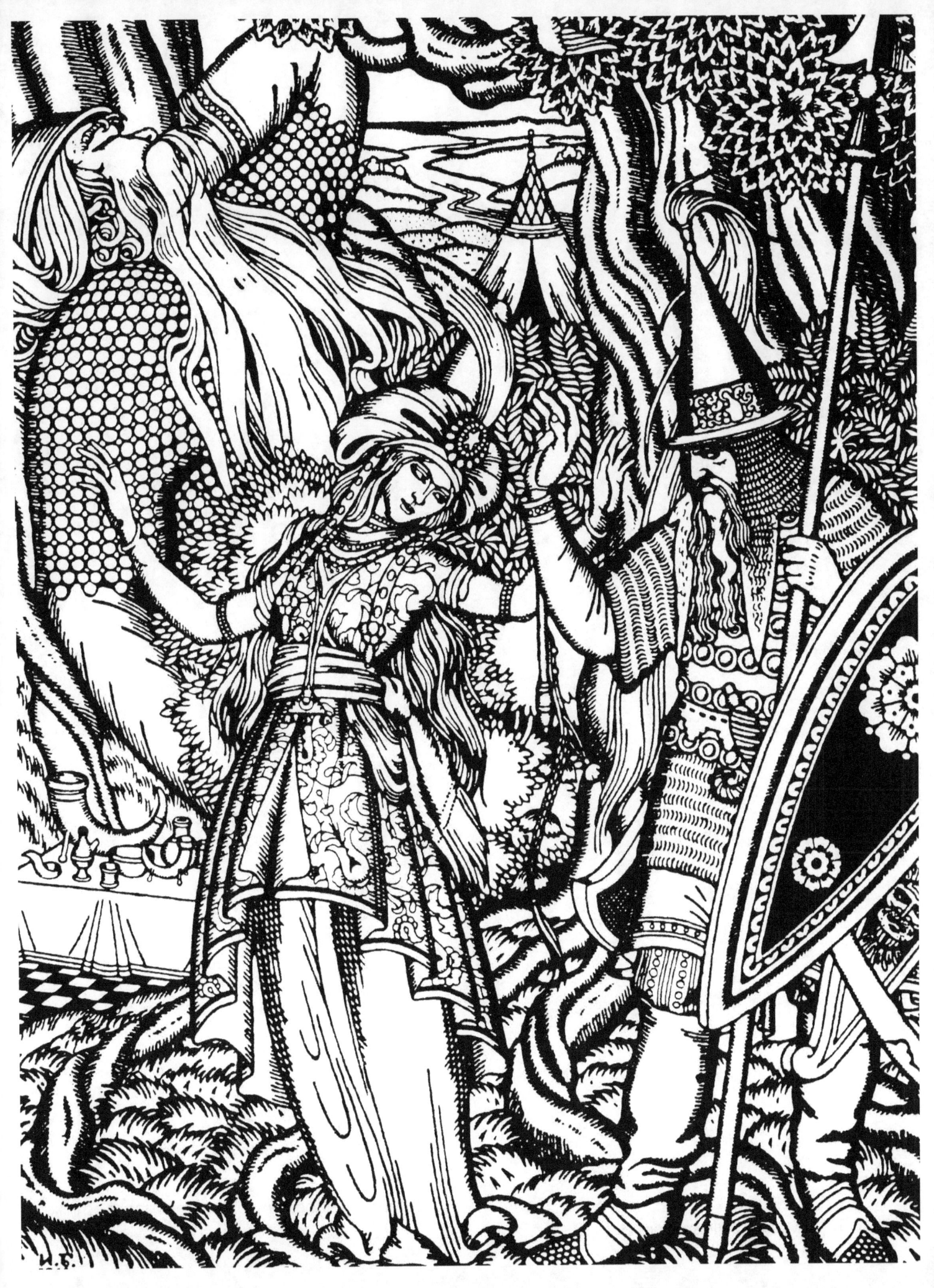

Ivan Bilibin
Russian Illustrator and Stage Director
1876-1942

Illustration for the Song of the Merchant Kalashnikov.

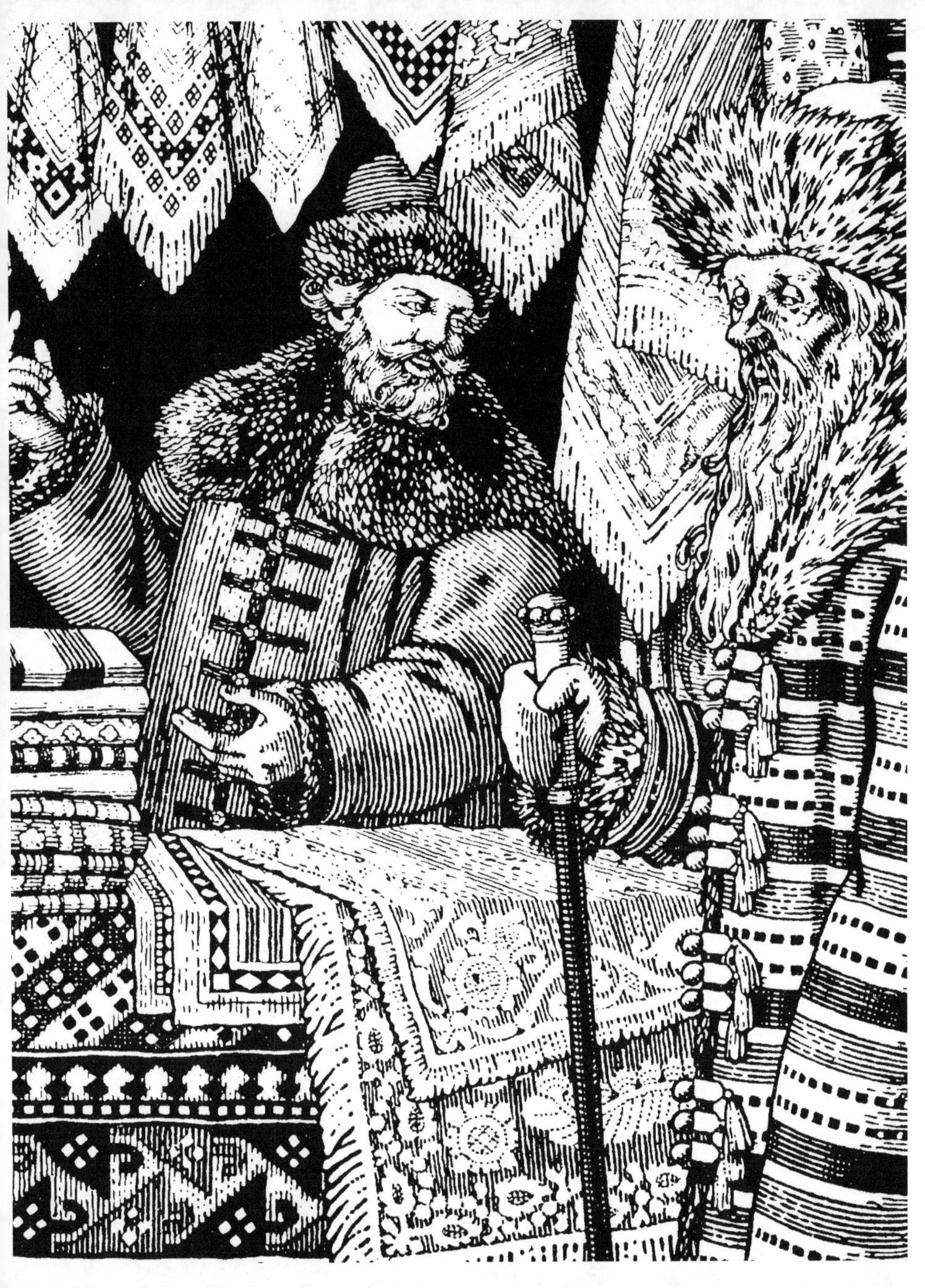

Ivan Bilibin
Russian Illustrator and Stage Director
1876-1942

Illustration for the Song of the Merchant Kalashnikov.

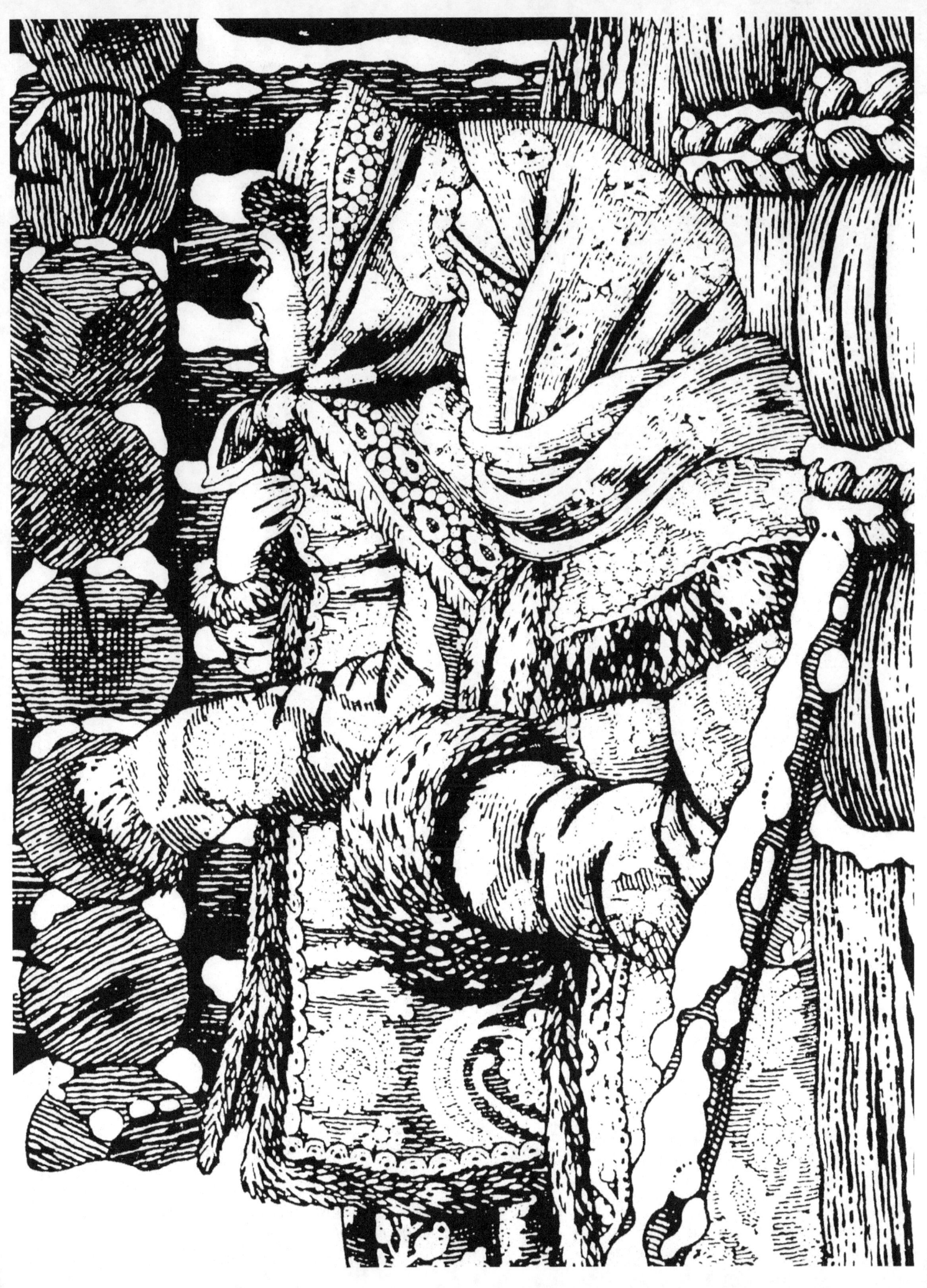

Harry Clarke
Irish Stained Glass Artist and Book Illustrator
1889-1931

This illustration is from *Tales of Mystery and Imagination* by Edgar Alan Poe.

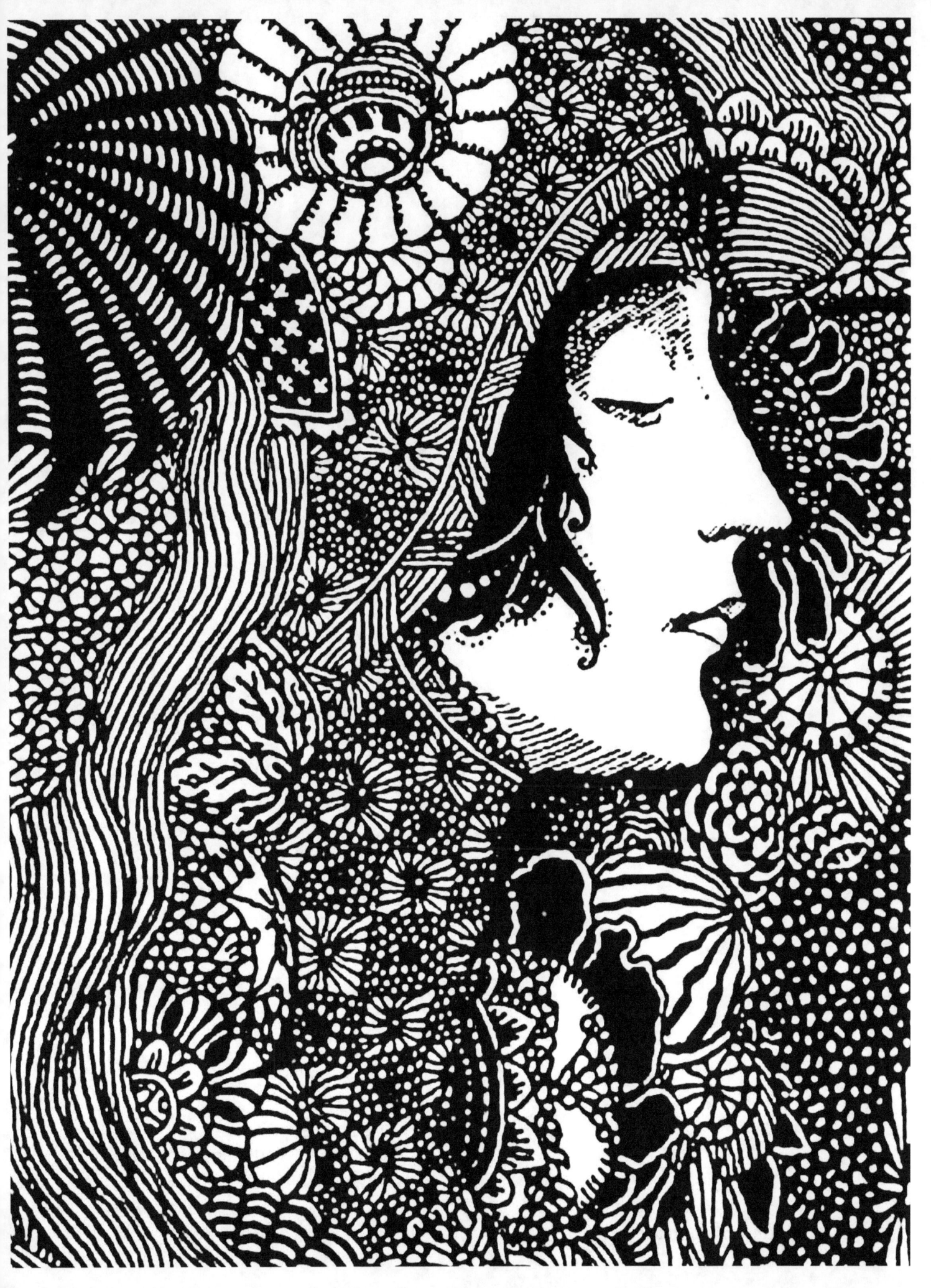

Harry Clarke
Irish Stained Glass Artist and Book Illustrator
1889-1931

This illustration is from *Tales of Mystery and Imagination* by Edgar Alan Poe.

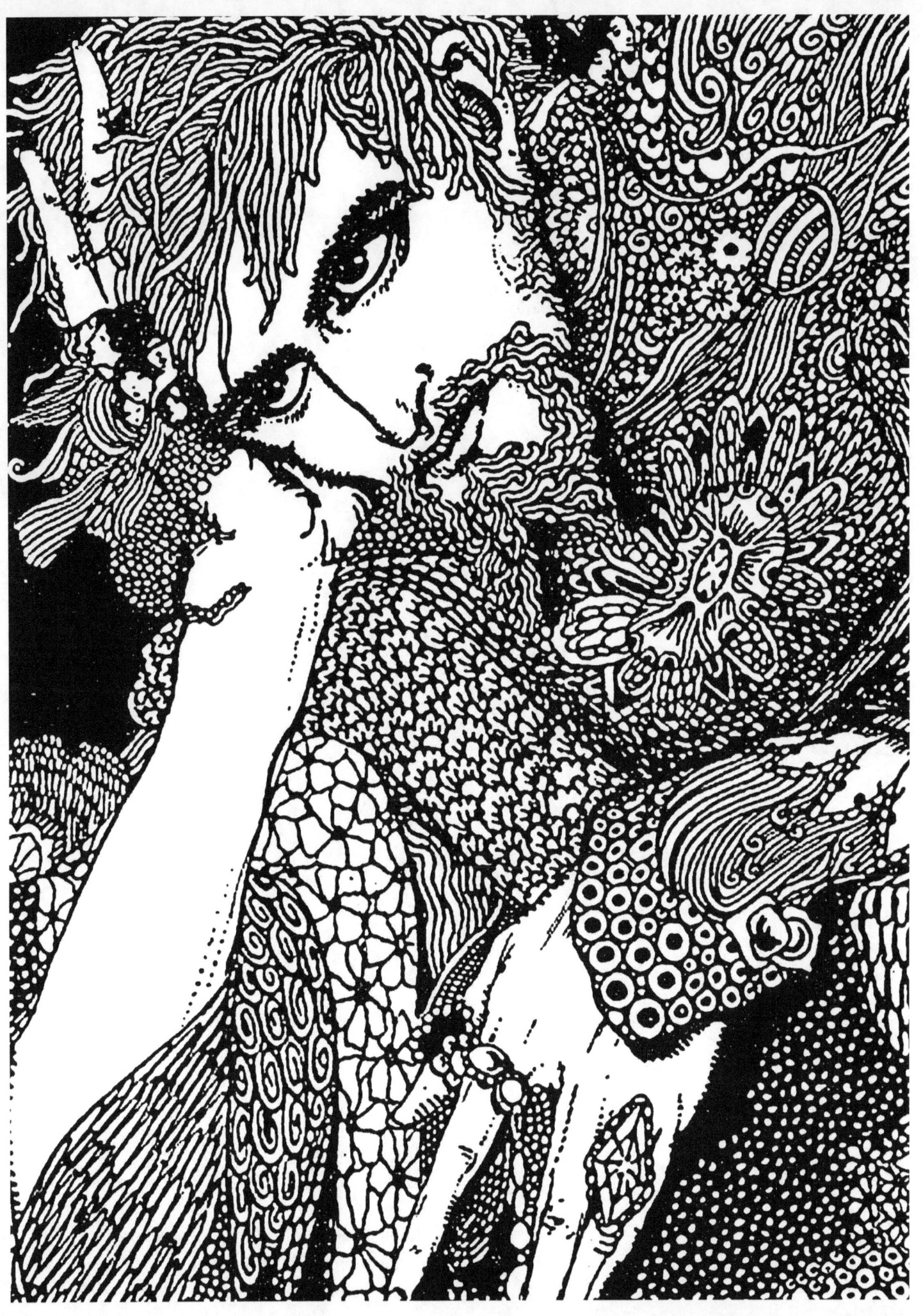

Harry Clarke
Irish Stained Glass Artist and Book Illustrator
1889-1931

This illustration is from *Tales of Mystery and Imagination* by Edgar Alan Poe.

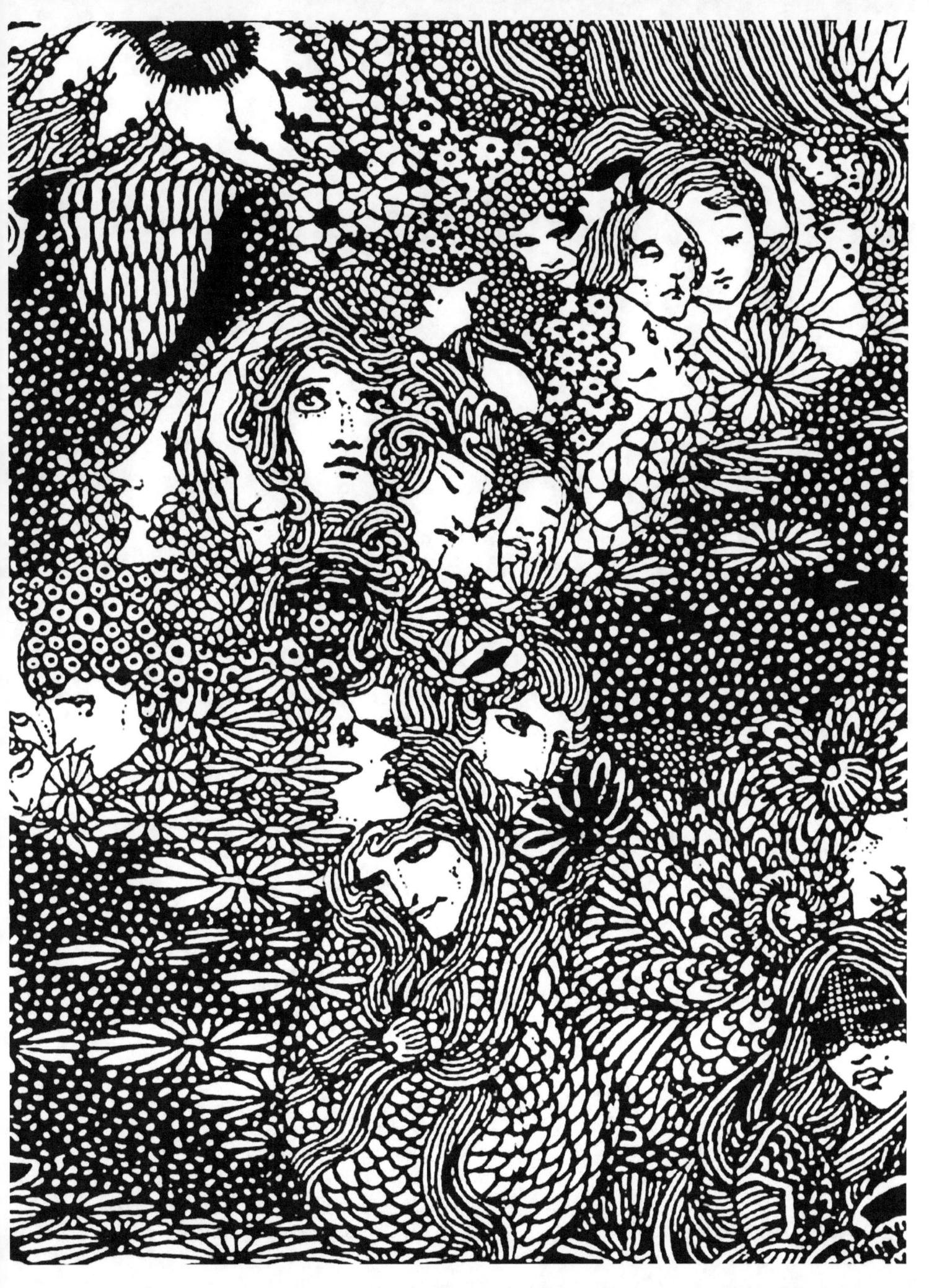

Harry Clarke
Irish Stained Glass Artist and Book Illustrator
1889-1931

This illustration is from *Tales of Mystery and Imagination* by Edgar Alan Poe.

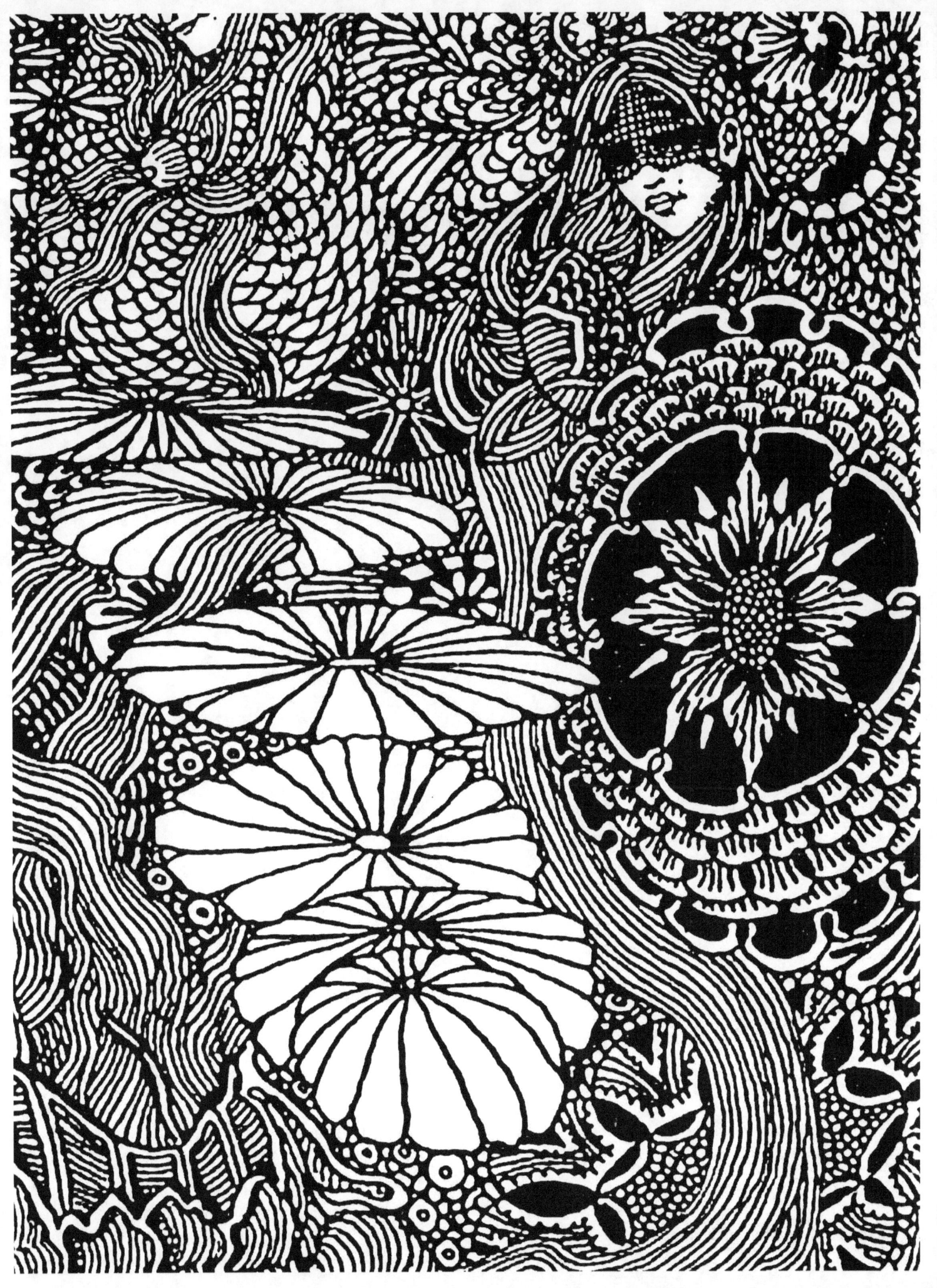

Harry Clarke
Irish Stained Glass Artist and Book Illustrator
1889-1931

This illustration is from *The Year's at the Spring*.

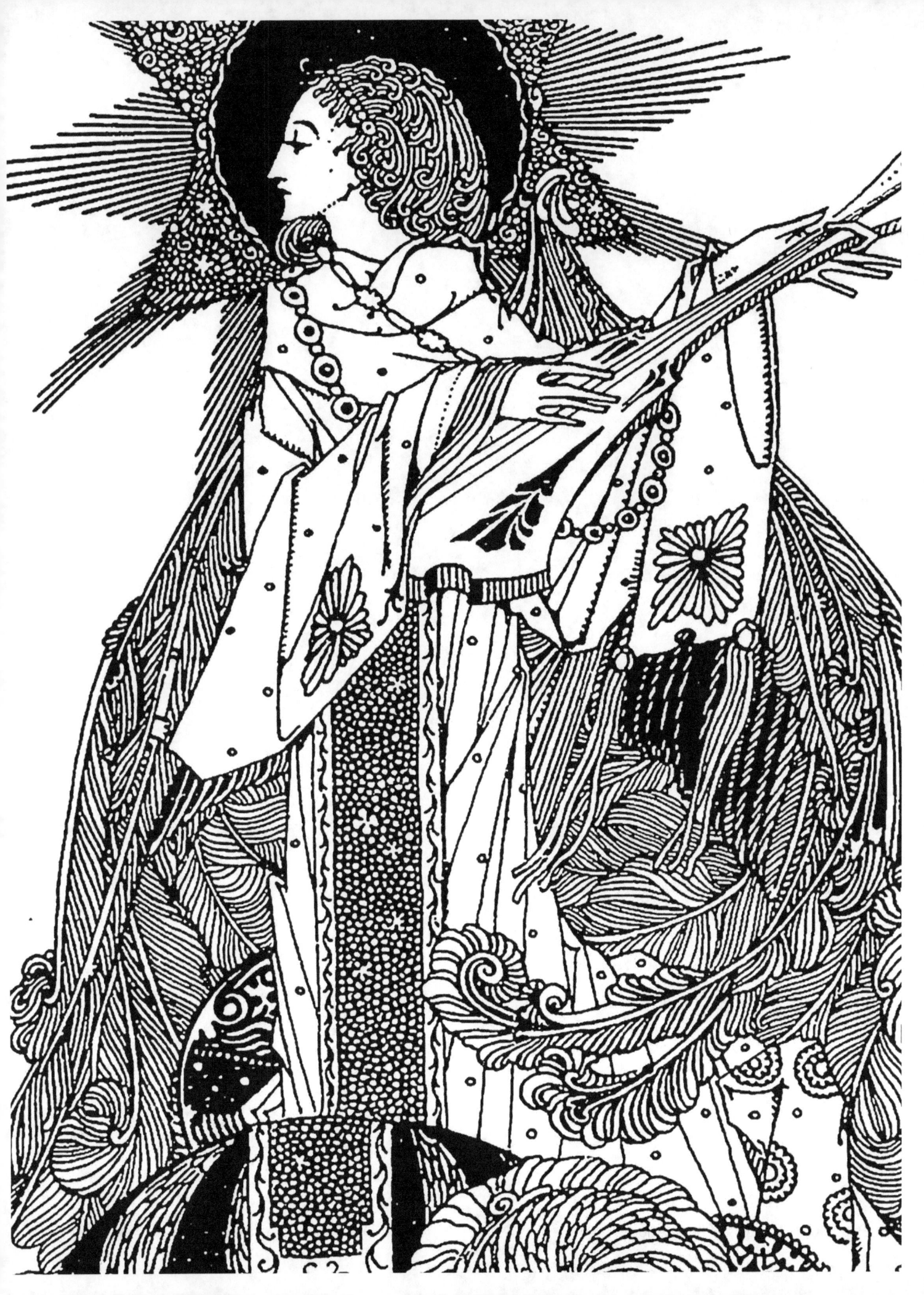

Henry Justice Ford
English Artist and Illustrator
1860-1941

This illustration is from *The Strong Prince* .

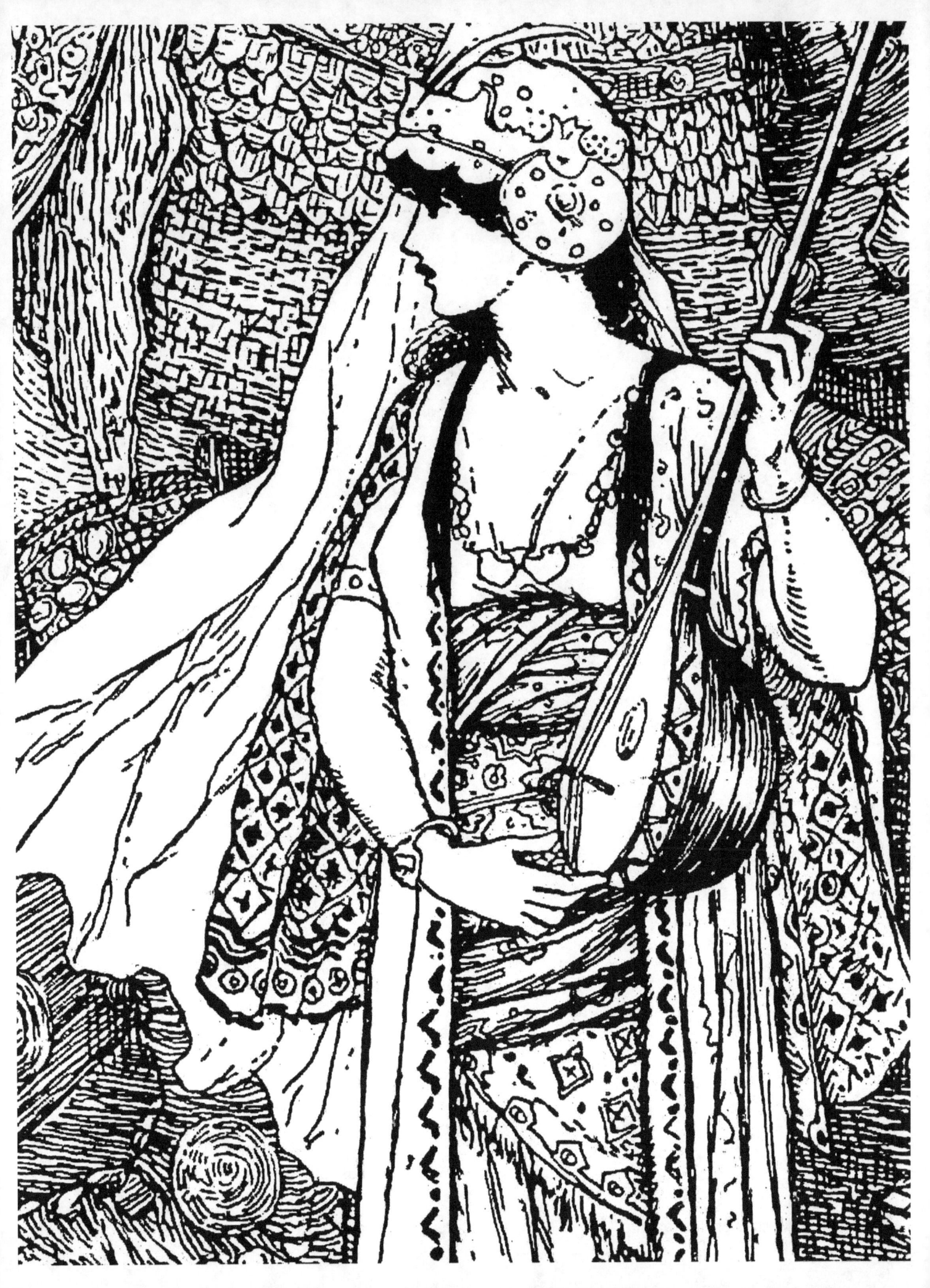

Joseph René Gockinga
Dutch Illustrator
1893-1962

Source unknown.

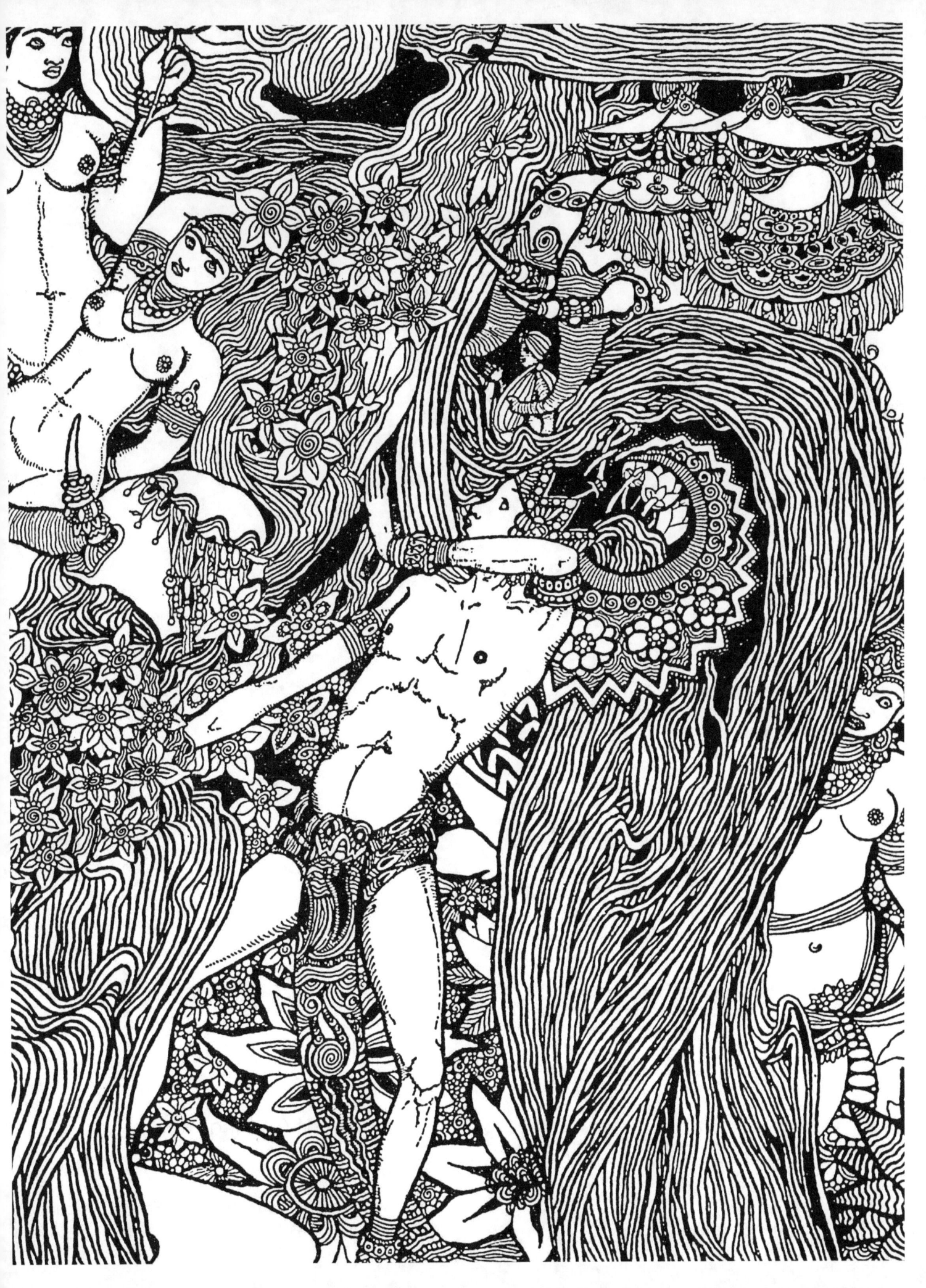

Joseph René Gockinga
Dutch Illustrator
1893-1962

From the Indonesian satirical-political periodical
De Zweep [The Whip] 1922.

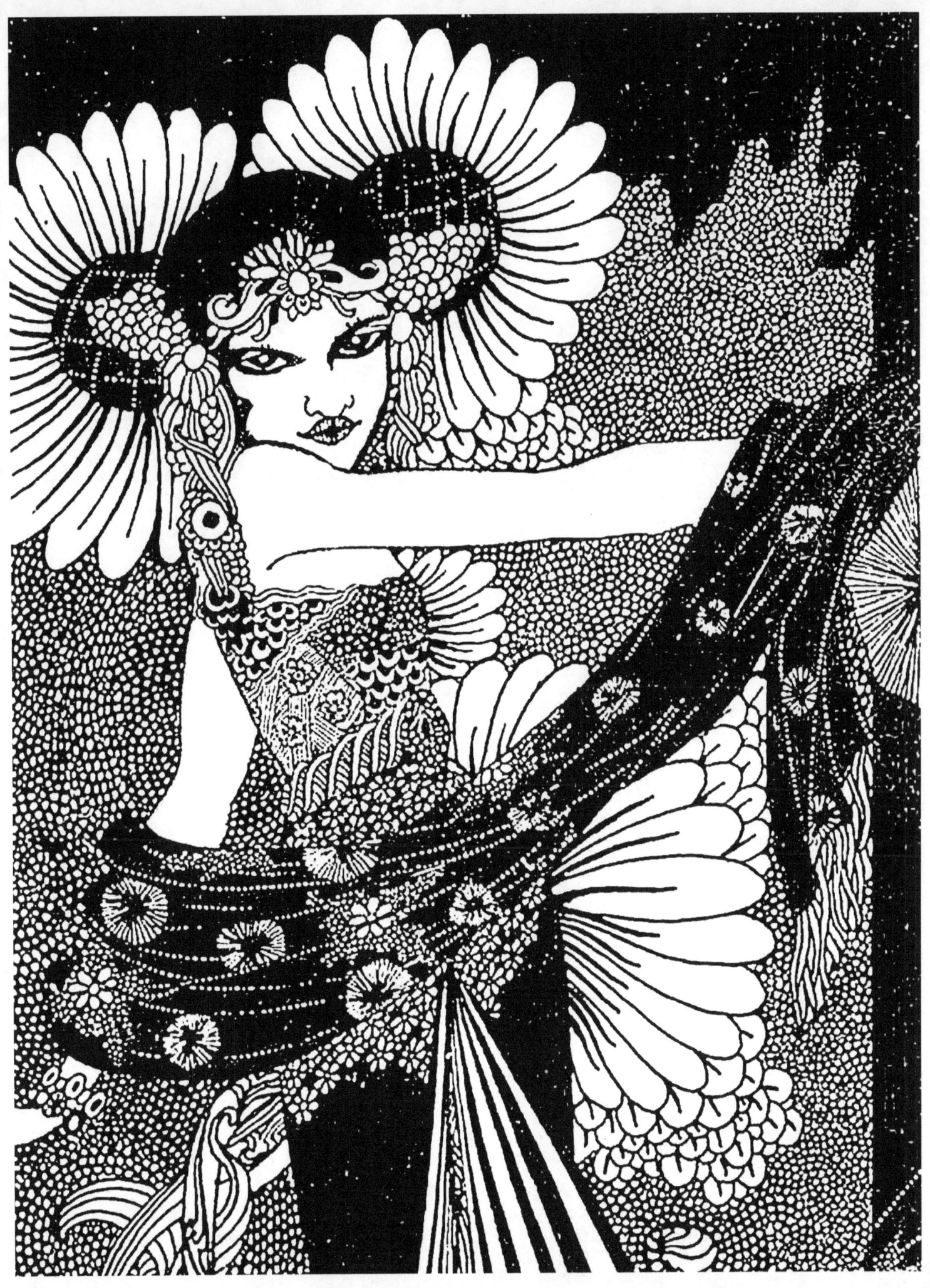

William Heath Robinson
English Cartoonist and Illustrator
1872-1944

This illustration is from *The Wild Swans*
by Hans Christian Andersen.

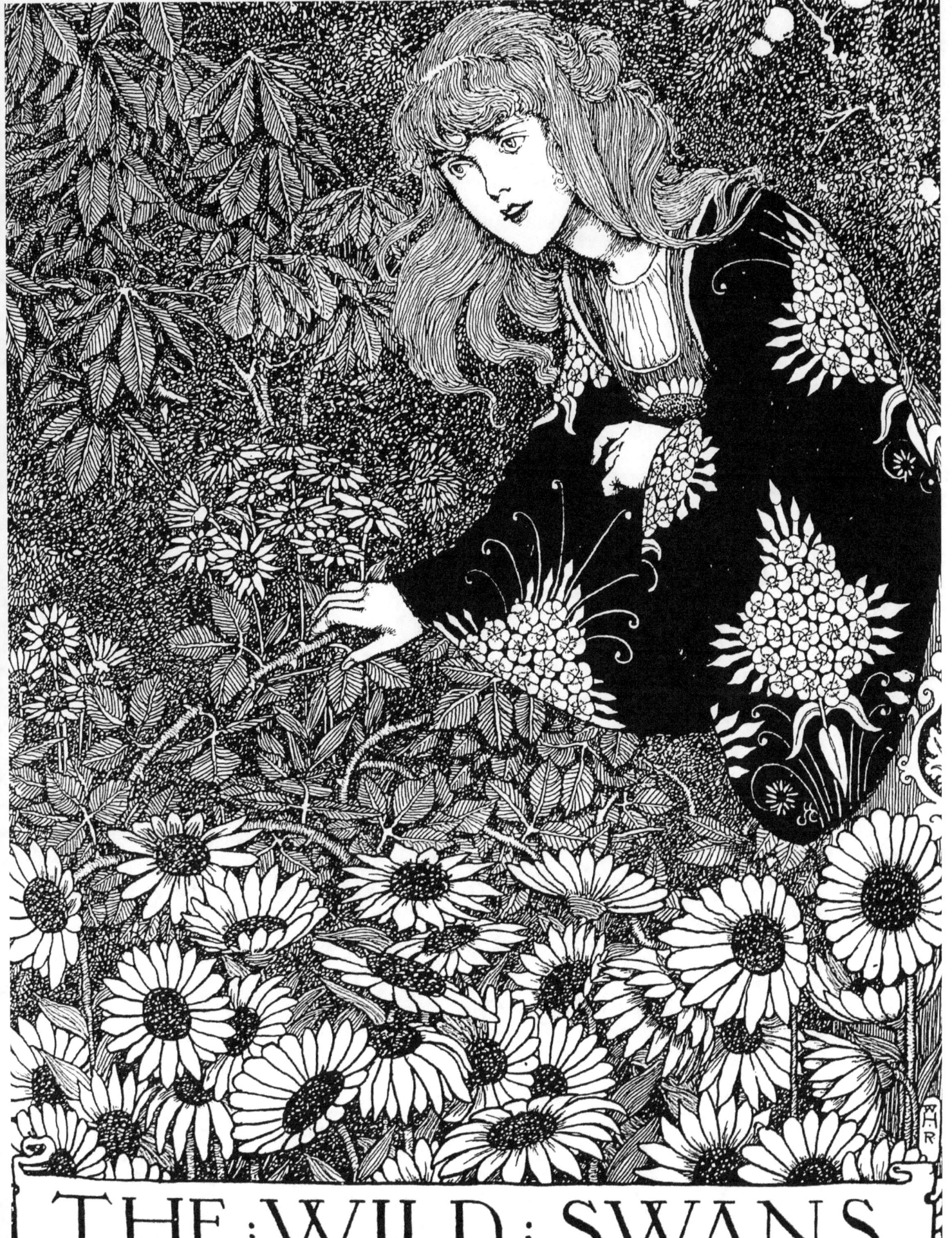

THE · WILD · SWANS

John Tenniel
English Book Illustrator knighted for his
achievements by Queen Victoria in 1893
1820-1914

This illustration is from *Alice's Adventures in
Wonderland by Lewis Carroll*

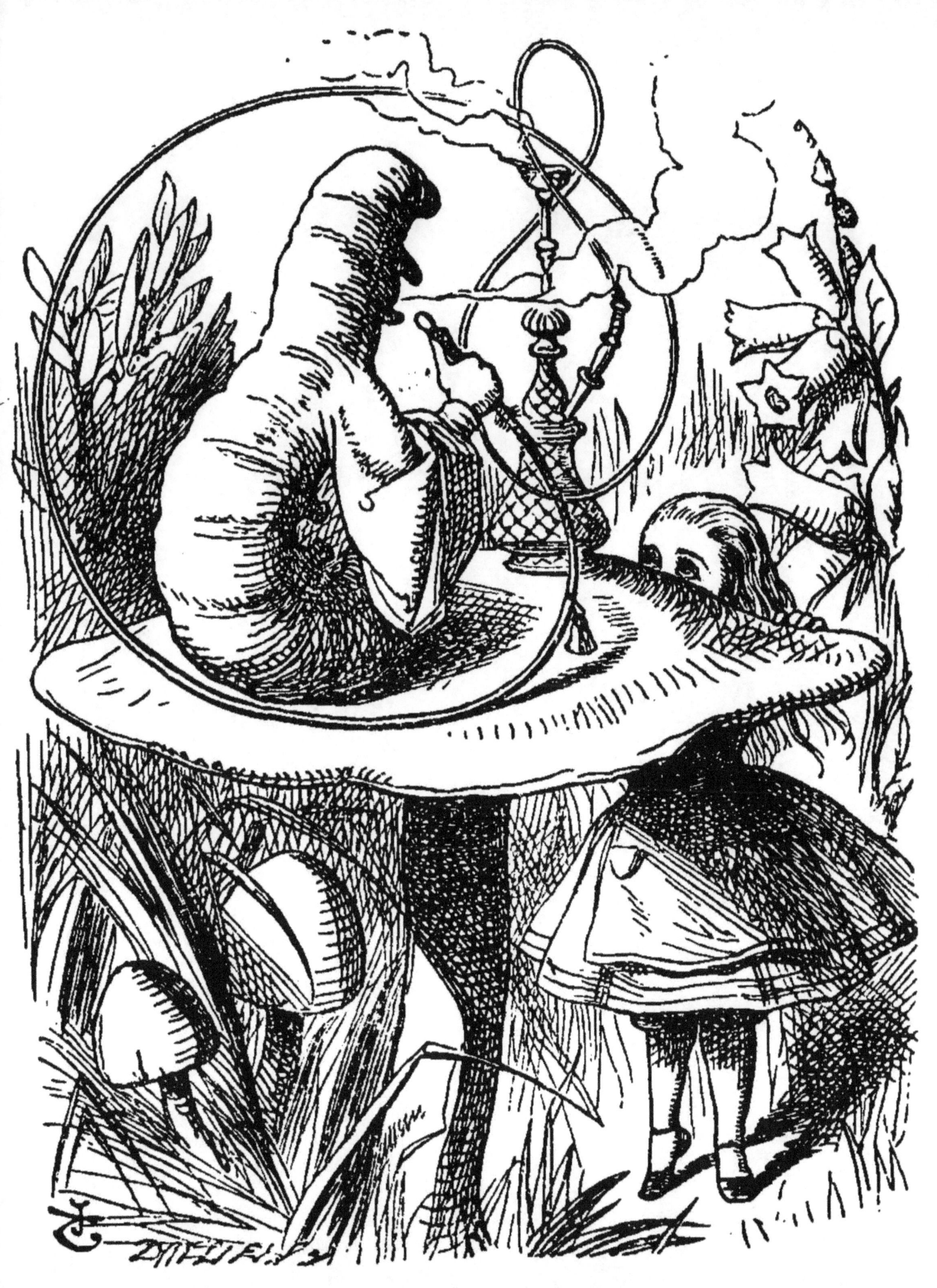

John Tenniel
English Book Illustrator knighted for his
achievements by Queen Victoria in 1893
1820-1914

This illustration is from *Alice's Adventures in
Wonderland by Lewis Carroll*

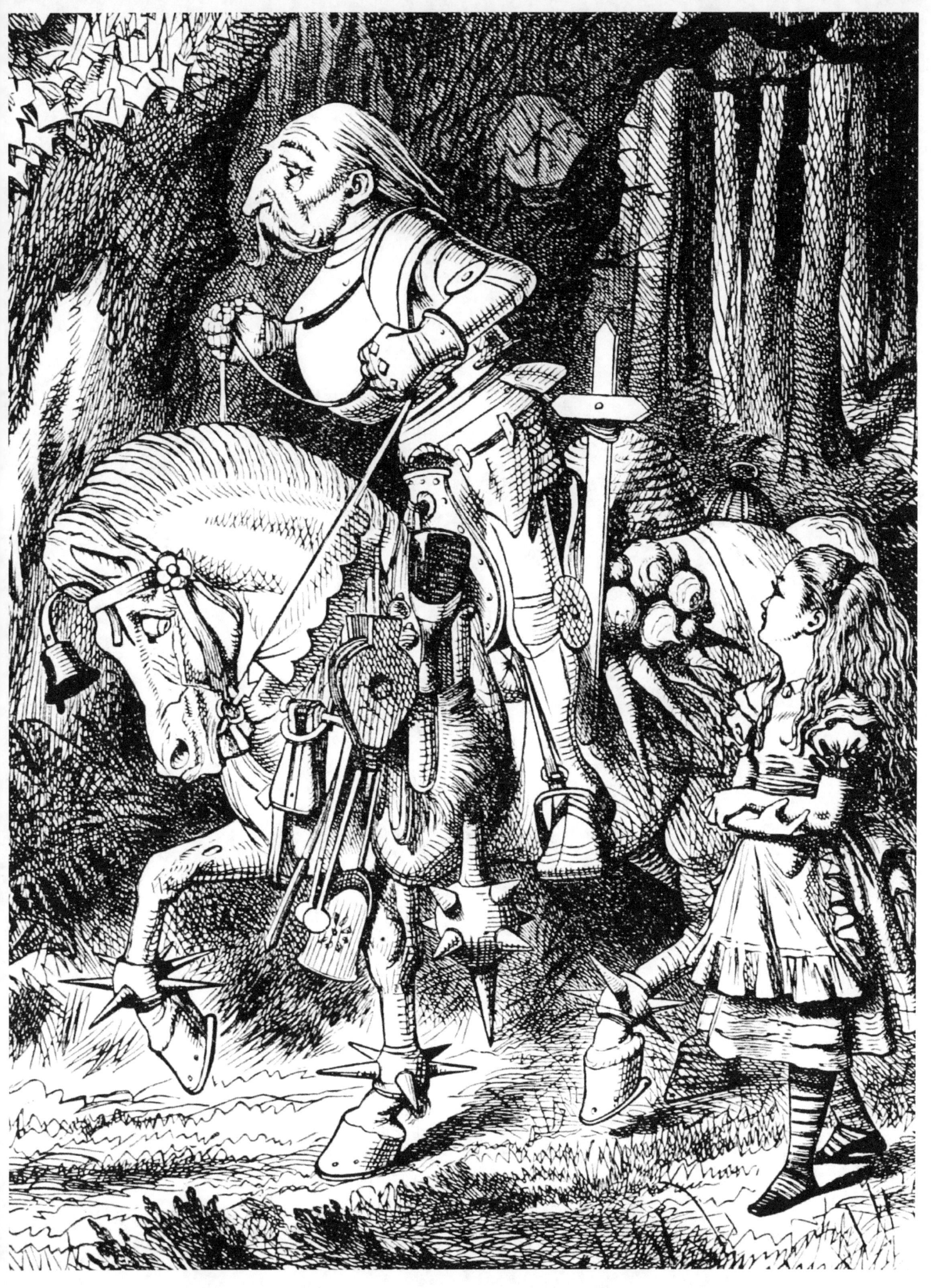

John Tenniel
English Book Illustrator knighted for his
achievements by Queen Victoria in 1893
1820-1914

This illustration is from *Alice's Adventures in
Wonderland by Lewis Carroll*

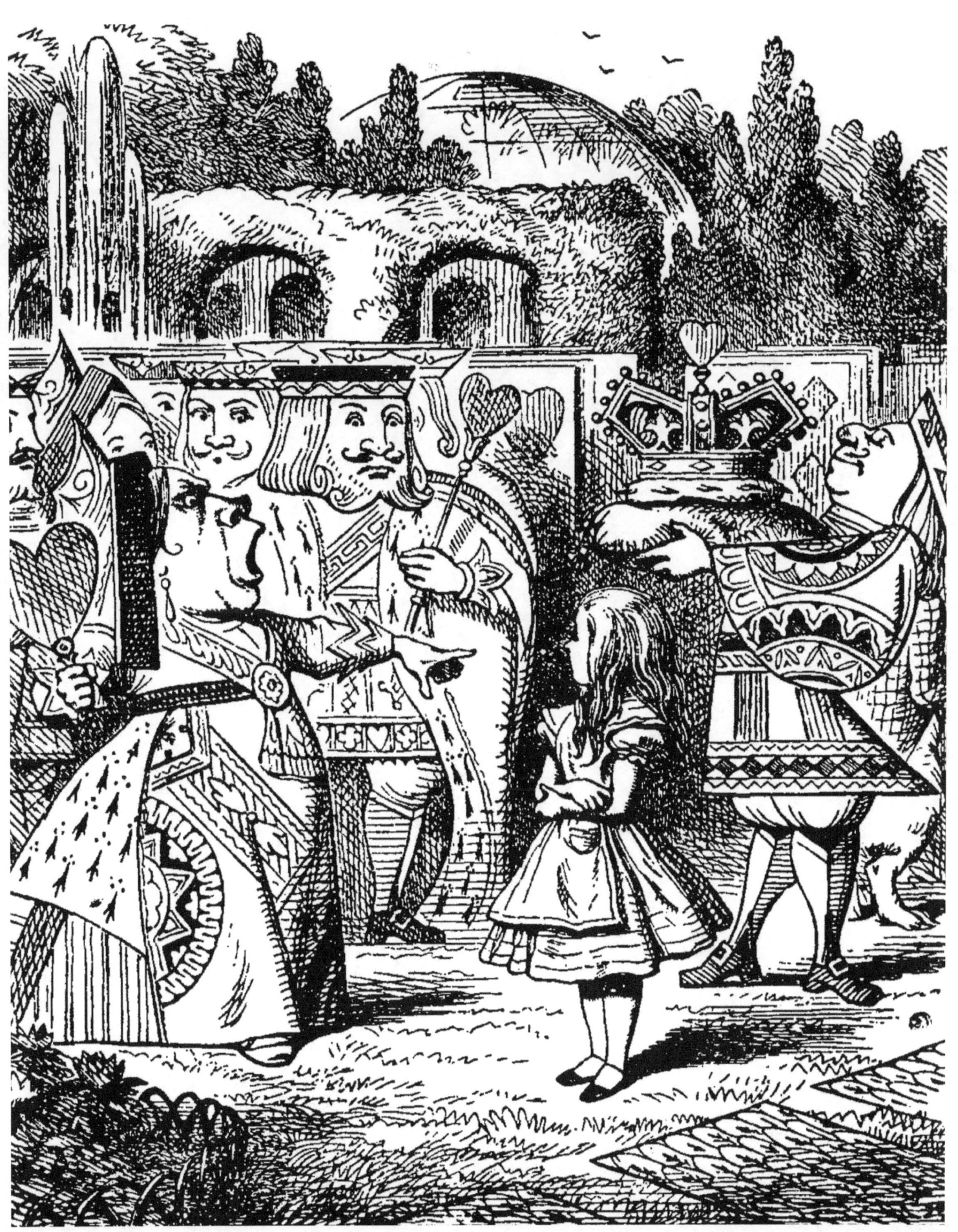

John Tenniel
English Book Illustrator knighted for his
achievements by Queen Victoria in 1893
1820-1914

This illustration is from *Alice's Adventures in
Wonderland by Lewis Carroll*

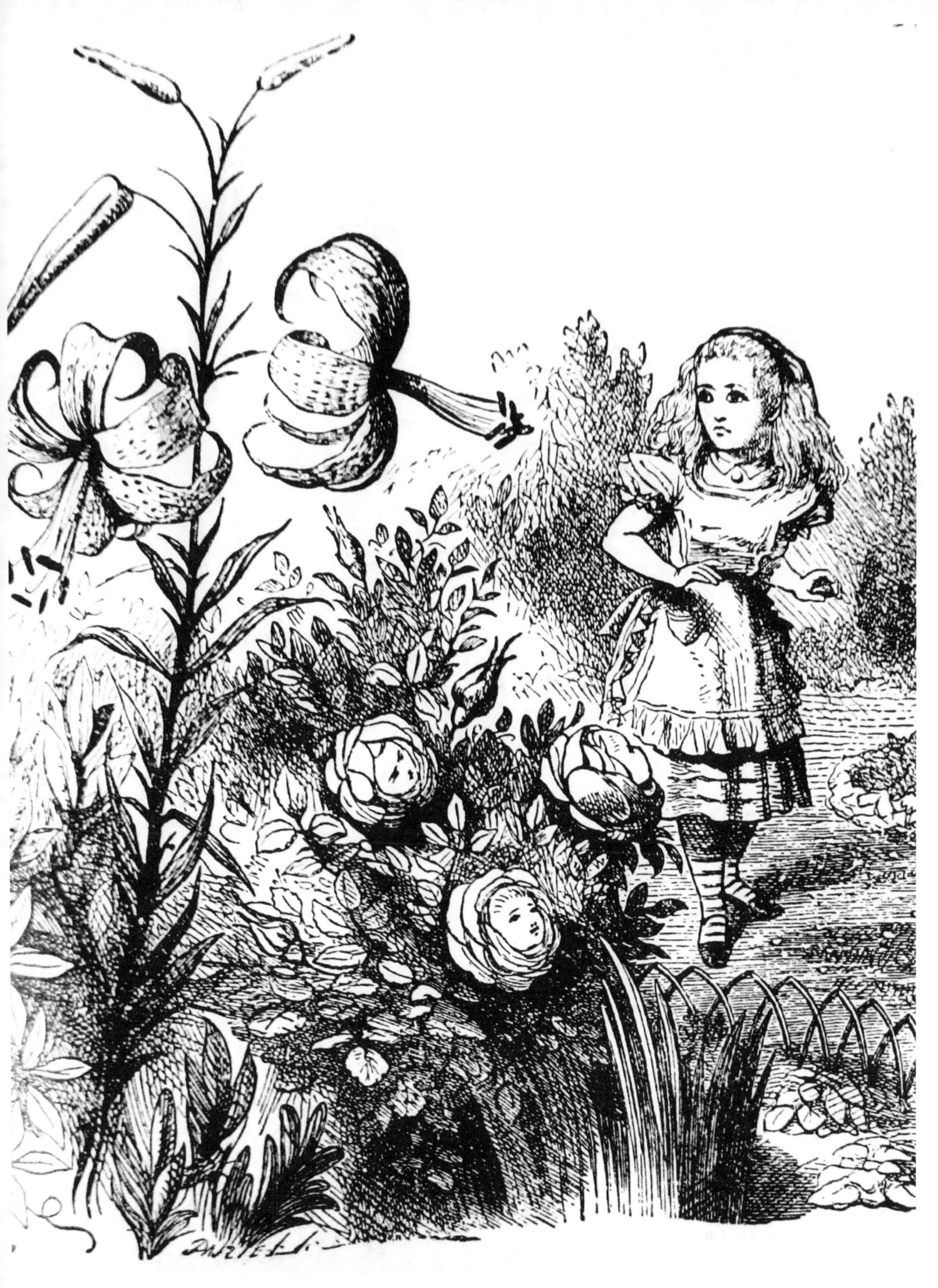

by Unknown

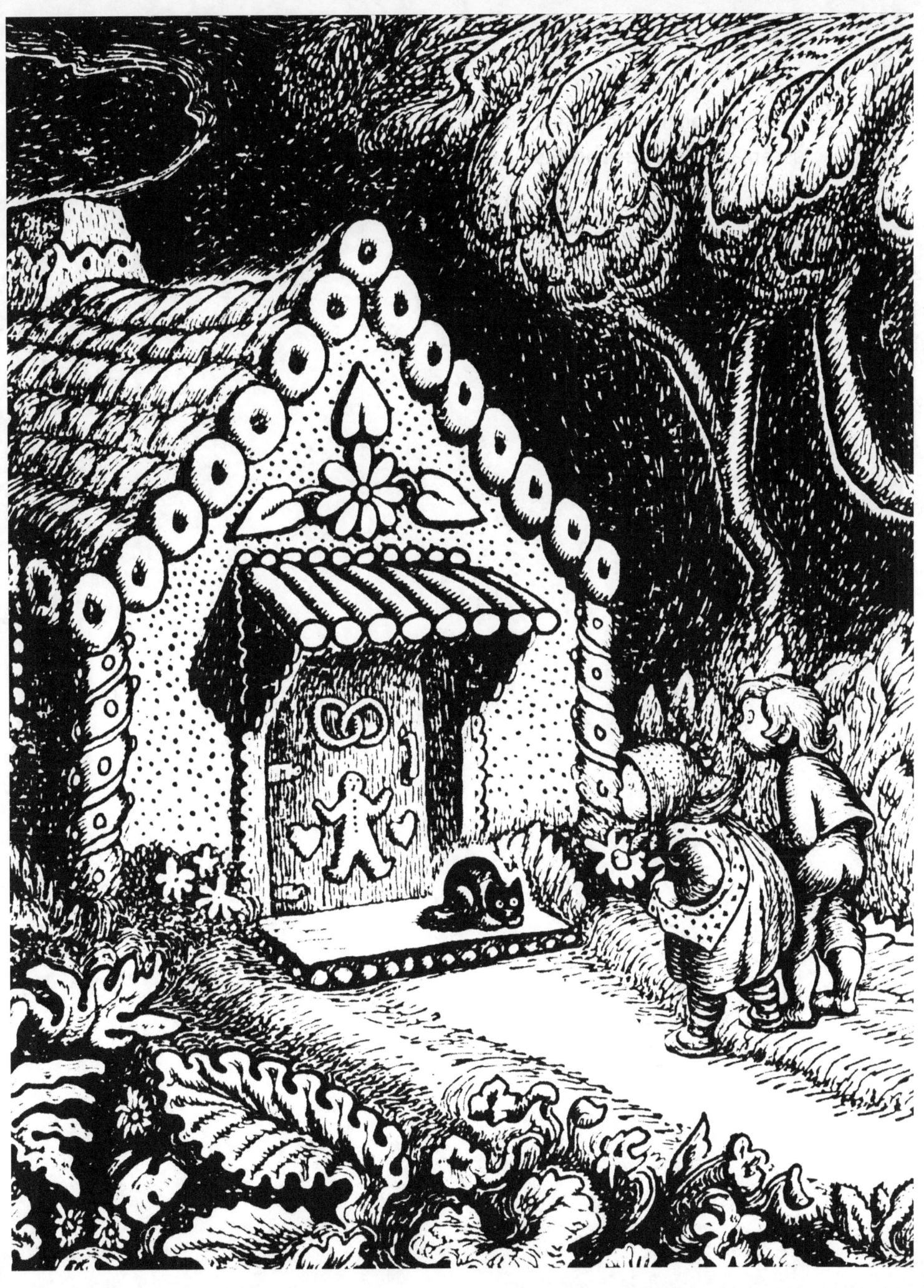

High resolution files for your digital coloring bliss are available by request.
Just email **colorspacebooks@gmail.com** and include this password: **PEACE**

Happy Coloring!